Christian Ho'oponopono Forgiveness Practice

Your Key to Forgiving Yourself,

Accepting God's Forgiveness,

Releasing Guilt and Fear,

And Finding Inner Peace

(FREE Bonus Meditation Download included with Book)

by
Angela Parish

Copyright © 2014 Angela Parish

All rights reserved.

ISBN-13: 978-1500641368
ISBN-10: 1500641367

DEDICATION

This book is lovingly dedicated to all those who sincerely seek a deeper understanding and acceptance of their own blessed sonship and daughtership as God's children.

ACKNOWLEDGMENTS

I would like to acknowledge the love and support of my spiritual study group. It was through the collective consciousness of many people that I came to know and use this beautiful Ho'oponopono practice.

CONTENTS

Preface	i
Introduction	1
Ho'oponopono: The Christian's Key to Forgiving	7
The Caveat — Responsibility	17
How to do The Christian Ho'oponopono Forgiveness Practice	21
Final Thoughts	27
Conclusion	29
About the Author	33
Bonus Offer: Free Meditation Download	35

PREFACE

As I looked at the picture in my hand, I saw the familiar face of a pretty, but shy, little 5-year-old. Her searching eyes stared back at me almost apologetically, her hesitant smile asking only if I could love her. I spoke the words of the Ho'oponopono Forgiveness Practice to her several times as instructed, and then passed the picture to the person next to me.

One by one, the pictures of the 40-some-odd participants passed into my hands. I looked at each photo while repeating the mantra we were given; there were boys and girls of various ages, colors, and sizes, each with a hidden story behind the eyes and smiles. Finally, my picture returned and I looked at it, expecting to see the prescient sadness of a child who would grow to adulthood carrying the sting of feeling not-quite-good-enough.

Yet in this picture, there was not the same little girl I prayed over almost an hour ago! No, this child's eyes sparkled with expectancy and her sweet smile belied a tender trust. A thrill went through me and tears welled in my eyes as I realized that the sadness, fear, and self-condemnation I had seen in this innocent face had come from within *me*! It had grown out of 50-plus years of my own fear, guilt and judgment! Why have I held myself in such contempt all these years? Where did it come from? Oh, it matters not! The past is dead! All wounds, whether self-inflicted or from someone else, are forgotten. I embrace a *new* me, one who is unfettered and who can unabashedly, shamelessly, and unapologetically dance and sing and live in pure joy!

Welcome to my new world! This is what I seek to share with you in this little book because I sincerely want you to know that you, too, can live a joyful life without shame, regrets or guilt. The Ho'oponopono Forgiveness Practice has made a huge, life-changing impact on my life and I want to present it in terms that speak personally to Christians, for it is a perfect method for living the message of Jesus Christ. I invite you to join me on this exciting, awesome journey with your heart open and expectant, for you will receive what you expect!

I wish I could show you,
When you are lonely or in darkness,
The astonishing light of your own being.

~

INTRODUCTION

The Hawaiian Ho'oponopono is a mental and emotional purification method that clears out fear, worry, and unhealthy relationship patterns in individuals, families and even whole communities. It also helps release religious dogmas and beliefs that oppose and prevent one's spiritual growth; and it removes deep and hidden mental and emotional blocks that manifest in the body as disease, depression and distress. The Ho'oponopono is a method that fosters mental, spiritual and emotional health and well-being.

The Ho'oponopono is based on the premise that God intends His creation to live in community with others in peace, joy and love. In familiar Christian terms, God is Love and wants us to receive and live in His Joy, Peace, and Love.

There are two components to the Ho'oponopono. The first component originated in the Polynesian islands and its origin is lost to antiquity. Later, in the 20th century, it was modified for modern society. The second component was developed in the 1990's by Ihaleakala Hew Len who was a student of Ho'oponopono.

The Ancient Hawaiian Ho'oponopono: Buried deeply within our subconscious are unresolved memories of past conflicts, hurt feelings and painful events and circumstances. These include family, community and racial memories that perpetuate strife and hatred between its members. These hidden memories affect how we act and react to current situations and relationships, and they will never go away on their own. They stay lodged in our psyches, unexpectedly surfacing in various aspects of our lives, including our bodies in the form of disease, until they are resolved and healed.

"The Family Feud": You, or someone you know, may have family members who have ceased talking to each other because of a misunderstanding or disagreement. You may even be among them. These feuds can last a lifetime, or many lifetimes, and often those involved forget, or don't even know, what started it. Neither side will give in and apologize first so the feud only continues.

Ancient Hawaiian lore tells of a certain tribal leader, called a *kahuna*, who developed the Ho'oponopono after he observed unresolved rifts and conflicts among his people, some of which had originated in a long forgotten generation. The *Kahuna* entrusted his shaman, or tribal holy man, to perform rituals and offer prayers and chanting to heal the conflicts and free his people from unconscious painful memories, thus allowing the tribe to regain its natural spiritual relationship with God and reclaim love and peace for its members.

The Modern Hawaiian Ho'oponopono: In the 1950's, the Hawaiian Elder, Mary Kawena Pukiu (1895-1986) expanded the Ho'oponopono by shifting the healing from the shaman into the hands of the people. She introduced family conferences where members would air their differences and work through conflicts and heal the rifts that had kept them apart. She refused to allow faultfinding or "finger-pointing"; individuals were required to take responsibility for and examine their own feelings and assumptions. Periods of silence allowed each person to reflect on his or her emotions, perceived injuries, anger, and resentment; and then through dialogue, they all aired their feelings and acknowledged those of the other members. Each person recognized and accepted his or her personal responsibility for the conflict. Thus, the whole family worked through and released all negative emotions, guilt, resentment and recriminations that had kept them divided and full of anger and hatred. They essentially cut out the past. The conference ended in a celebration and feast with everyone re-embracing brotherly love and emotional health.

In the early 1990's, Ihaleakala Hew Len added a second component to the Ho'oponopono by introducing the mantra, "I'm sorry. Please forgive me. I love you. Thank you." Len based the mantra on the premise that each individual is responsible for creating his or her emotional and mental pain in any situation. In other words, anytime someone offends you, you should recognize that it is not the other person's action that upset you but an unresolved or unhealed memory within your subconscious that was triggered, which then caused you to take offense.

Len taught that whenever you feel yourself becoming upset about something or someone, you silently repeat the first two phrases, "I'm sorry. Please forgive me." You are saying these phrases to *yourself* for any negative actions or reactions you are having toward the person or situation, or harsh words you may have spoken to the other person. You also mentally direct the two phrases to anyone else involved in the situation for the effect your actions or words may have had on him or her.

Then you say the next two phrases of the mantra silently as well, "I love you. Thank you." You are also saying this to yourself and to the other person or persons. You surrender and accept what your intellect does not know — that the perfect and right solution for all problems is within your heart.

The Ho'oponopono Forgiveness technique may sound too simple or appear ineffective, but it is a powerful technique that, when used consistently, will quickly bring about changes in your life. Use it whenever you encounter a person or situation that makes you uncomfortable, fearful, or feel guilty. Always accept responsibility for your *feelings* and *reactions* to whatever occurs in your life. You may not have any control over someone or something, but you can control how you feel and react toward that person or situation.

For more information on the Hawaiian Ho'oponopono, I highly recommend *Ho'oponopono: The Hawaiian Forgiveness Ritual as the Key to Your Life's Fulfillment* by Ulrich E. Dupree.

Ho'oponopono for Christians: From a Christian standpoint, repeating the words, "I am sorry, please forgive me, I love you, thank you," helps you stay centered in Christ's Love within your heart and keeps you from reacting negatively to what someone says or does to you or anything that is happening around you.

The Ho'oponopono does not put you in a position of weakness but of incredible power — the Christ power within you. It is also an exceptionally effective process for helping you begin to forgive yourself, and allow you to forgive others and release deep-seated resentment, anger and emotional pain.

Yet, let's be clear about one thing. The Ho'oponopono does not justify someone abusing you. It does not mean that you should allow anyone to hurt you physically or emotionally; in that situation you should remove yourself from that person immediately. The Christian Ho'oponopono

Forgiveness Practice presented later in this book will help you heal the deep wounds you received from any and all situations.

Clearing our hearts and minds of mental and emotional pain allows us to receive the forgiveness that Jesus Christ promised us, to accept ourselves as the divine children God created us to be, and to live in peace and harmony with others. By using the four Ho'oponopono phrases and the Christian Ho'oponopono Forgiveness Practice presented later in this book, you will be embarking on an exciting journey to healing and wholeness in Christ.

HO'OPONOPONO:
THE CHRISTIAN'S KEY TO FORGIVING

So, why this book, *Christian Ho'oponopono Forgiveness Technique*? Why would a Christian be at all interested in the Ho'oponopono forgiveness technique? Isn't this frowned upon by the church? Is this sacrilegious?

Absolutely not! And I'll tell you why.

One of the foremost messages of Jesus when he walked and taught on this earth was the importance of forgiveness.

> **Psalm 103:8-12** *The LORD is merciful and gracious, slow to anger and abounding in steadfast love. He will not always chide, nor will he keep his anger forever. He does not deal with us according to our sins, nor repay us according to our iniquities. For as high as the heavens are above the earth, so great is his steadfast love toward those who fear him; as far as the east is from the west, so far does he remove our transgressions from us.*

> **Isaiah 1:18** *"Come now, let us reason together, says the LORD: though your sins are like scarlet, they shall be as white as snow; though they are red like crimson, they shall become like wool.*
>
> **Luke 7:47-48** *"...Therefore I tell you, her sins, which are many, are forgiven — for she loved much. But he who is forgiven little, loves little." And he said to her, "Your sins are forgiven." (Jesus speaking to the accusers and the woman caught in adultery.)*

As children, our parents and Sunday school teachers told us to love our enemies and forgive anyone who hurts us because that is what the Bible teaches us. However, they didn't tell us exactly *how* to accomplish this feat, probably because they didn't know themselves. And what seemed impossible when we were children is no easier when we are grown up. As adults, we still find it difficult to forgive (and all but impossible to love) those who have hurt us deeply, much less our enemies. Though we may sincerely try, we usually fail just as when we were children. At best, we can only give lip service to it or blame our "human nature."

Does God really punish us for not being able to forgive? Yet, Jesus does not allow the "human nature" excuse. He made it clear that we must forgive others if we are to be forgiven. Apparently, He didn't think it was humanly impossible like some people do.

> *For if you forgive other people when they sin against you, your heavenly Father will also forgive you. But if you do not forgive others their sins, your Father will not forgive your sins.* Mark 6:14-15

The Merriam Webster Dictionary's definition of forgive is "to give up resentment of; to grant relief from payment of (as in debt); to cease to feel resentment against." Therefore, when one forgives, he lets go of anger, animosity, indignation, revenge and all those emotions that keep one stuck in a dead, "in the past," situation.

But let's understand one important point — forgiving others is not for God! Forgiving others does not win points for you, or blessings or special favors from your Father. God made it clear: Unless you forgive others, you cannot *receive* His forgiveness. He *already* loves you — His greatest pleasure is to "give you the Kingdom." Yet, resentment, anger, and feelings of revenge fill you with deep, dark emotions that prevent you from accepting and receiving what God *has already given you!*

Another thing our parents and teachers did not teach us when we were children is that we should *forgive ourselves*. Uh oh, I can hear you now — "Forgive myself?! What do you mean? Isn't that what Jesus is supposed to do?! I can't forgive myself, that's gotta be a sin or something."

Let me warn you: I will tell you several times in this little book — *your Father has already forgiven your sins!* When you accepted Jesus Christ into your heart, He completely forgave and forgot your sins — as if they never happened. Yet, unless you let go of resentment and until you can completely forgive others, you erect a wall between yourself and God that prevents you from accepting His forgiveness. And forgiving others includes forgiving yourself.

Can I really forgive myself? It's not easy to forgive yourself, much less love yourself. In fact, it may be more difficult to forgive yourself than to forgive someone else. Who hasn't done something in the past that they truly regret? Unfortunately, as you know, there is no rewind button to push to go back and do it over. There is no way to remove the past hurt that we have caused someone, or the shame we have brought to others and ourselves. Ah, but we *can* replay it in our heads over and over, never letting ourselves forget, and we can continually beat ourselves up for it, sing the blues, and wonder why we are so miserable. Not exactly a formula for a happy, emotionally healthy life, but we don't believe we deserve one anyway.

We all carry regrets and subconscious guilt that color our whole personality. Yet, there is an even more subtle, hidden influence on our lives — those forgotten memories of things we were told when we were very young: sharp words from a sibling, parent or schoolmate when we were too young to filter out the untruths; words that made us believe we were not good enough, pretty enough, or smart enough; words that told us we didn't or couldn't measure up to someone else's standards; maybe it was an accident or event that we believed was our fault. We carry these forgotten memories in our subconscious for decades and they prevent us from living and expressing the wonderful, divine qualities God had freely given us.

Does the Bible tell us to forgive ourselves? There is considerable controversy in the Christian community about the idea of forgiving oneself. Some ministers and Christians point out that the Bible says nothing about self-forgiveness, and they insist that forgiving yourself causes you to turn away from God, become selfish and vain, focusing only on yourself. Some ministers insist that forgiving oneself is sinful, that it creates a society of self-centered people and fosters violence and hatred.

Yet, on the contrary, forgiving yourself in no way implies that you expect others to put your affairs before theirs. It does not mean that you do not need God, Christ or the Holy Spirit, or that you do not need to love your Father in Heaven with all your heart. It does not give you permission to commit immoral, illegal or selfish acts. And self-forgiveness certainly does not give one license to hurt others.

Being able to forgive yourself is purely a personal thing between you and *yourself*. Continuing to punish yourself long after you have made restitution for something in the past only prevents you from living your life freely and fully today; and if you have not made restitution for a past mistake, it further deepens your guilt and remorse. Rather than putting God first in your life, holding onto guilt and pain and continuously punishing yourself actually keeps you focused on yourself.

In truth, forgiving yourself allows you to turn your attention away from yourself, no longer placing your needs above others. By letting go of guilt for past transgressions, you can then unashamedly open yourself to God and become a conduit of His love, easily sharing it with those around you because you deeply know that God's blessings are unlimited. You can love God and develop a relationship with the Holy Spirit when you forgive yourself, forget the past and let go of crippling guilt.

"Dear friends, if our hearts do not condemn us, we have confidence before God and receive from him anything we ask, because we keep his commands and do what pleases him." 1 John 21-22

The purpose of the Christian Ho'oponopono Forgiveness Practice is to forgive yourself and help you let go of painful feelings of unworthiness. It opens your heart to receive God's forgiveness and frees you to "live and move and have your being" in a continual relationship with the Holy Spirit and the Savior, Jesus Christ. And when you forgive yourself and know you are loved, you will then love yourself.

To love yourself is not self-centered or vain; it is not thinking that you are better than anyone. To love yourself does not mean that you expect everyone to give you what you want, or that your needs come before others'. No, to love yourself means you respect yourself; that you need not please someone at the expense of your safety or self-worth. You appreciate what you have — your God-given talents and abilities; you know that you are valuable to Him. To love yourself unconditionally allows you to accept others' love and freely return their love in a bond of brotherly love. You stop condemning yourself and anyone else because you know that we are all here trying to live our lives the best we can, maintaining faith that God recognizes our sincere efforts and loves us unconditionally.

In today's modern religious arenas, many church leaders recognize what psychologists have known for decades: that having a positive self-image — that is, loving and appreciating who you are — is tantamount to living an emotionally healthy and productive life.

When you use the four Ho'oponopono phrases and the Christian Ho'oponopono Forgiveness Practice, you stop condemning yourself for mistakes you deeply regret. They are in the past, and the past will not change no matter how tenaciously you hold onto it.

Biblical Support for the Christian Ho'oponopono Forgiveness Practice – When the prodigal son returned home, his father did not wait for him to crawl back to him in remorse. No, his father met him halfway and then immediately called for a banquet, bestowing onto his son all of the young man's intended inheritance.

The Bible tells us that it is God's greatest pleasure to give us the Kingdom, and just as the prodigal son's father, God gives to each of us without measure. What is the Kingdom? It is love of family, it is enjoyment of God's abundance and prosperity in life, and it is our unique talents and abilities that we can use for our own pleasure and to uplift others. It is also a deep and continuous relationship with Him through the Holy Spirit. However, carrying past guilt and remorse prevents us from accepting our rightful "inheritance," just as the prodigal son stayed away from his father because he could not believe he was worthy to receive the riches that were already his.

The only way we can accept God's forgiveness and unconditional love — His Kingdom — is to release those feelings of guilt, fear, and unworthiness that prevent us from forgiving ourselves.

Unclean, unclean! Consider the woman in Luke 8:43-48 who touched the hem of Jesus' robe. Here was a woman who had hemorrhaged blood for twelve years and Jewish law considered her unclean, or impure. The unclean could not participate in any public activities until they became clean, unclean women could not to have relations with their husbands, and all were forced into isolation from their families and communities. This woman had desperately tried every doctor and remedy she could find but to no avail, depleting her physically, spiritually and financially. Living alone and ostracized as an untouchable was dreadfully demeaning and devastating.

The unclean could be killed immediately if they accidentally touched someone; therefore, whenever they were in public or around other people, the law required them to announce continuously to everyone "Unclean, unclean." So by pushing through the crowd to see Jesus, the woman was risking her life to be healed and made whole.

We would never think of treating our friends or family like that. Yet, frequently, because we suffer from our own deep shame and guilt, we subconsciously announce to all whom we meet, "Unclean, unclean," and we hold back from fully giving ourselves to those most dear to us. Past guilt and memories of things we heard when very young, or financial, marital or family problems we have today can prevent us from living life unashamedly.

The woman's faith in Jesus Christ healed her, yet, many of us, no matter how many times we hear that we, too, are healed through Jesus Christ, cannot accept His love because of our deeply held sense of unworthiness and "uncleanness."

Jesus Christ came to earth to save those who believe in Him from the grip of eternal death, and any Christian who sincerely asks the Father to forgive his or her sins is unconditionally forgiven. As Christians, we can use the Christian Ho'oponopono Forgiveness Practice presented in this book to heal ourselves and allow ourselves to accept and receive the promise of glory that the Lord Jesus Christ gave us.

How Can I Forgive Someone Else Who Hurt Me So Deeply? Many of us have been hurt deeply by those who should have given us love and nurturing. Usually, this was at a very young age when we were unable to defend ourselves. So, how can one heal from such deep pain and wounds? How can we begin to heal from such trauma?

Jesus did not give any special conditions that absolve us from having to forgive others. Yet some situations seem all but impossible. The Christian Ho'oponopono Forgiveness Practice is a powerful method that can begin healing those deep emotional, mental and physical wounds from past trauma.

Important: If the abuse was serious and the hurt prevents you from living a normal life, you should not hesitate to seek professional counseling. You can use the Christian Ho'oponopono Forgiveness Practice with any other treatment you may seek.

Can you accept God's unconditional love? Have you ever known someone who seemed absolutely carefree in their personal faith and actions, always expecting and receiving the best that life offers? Have you ever wondered how they are able to live so effortlessly? Are they free of "sin"? Have they been able to accept Christ's forgiveness, and if so, how?

When you use the Christian Ho'oponopono Forgiveness Practice and start forgiving yourself, you begin almost immediately to live the way that you have only imagined. You become that carefree person you have so longed to be. Not only will you know and accept God's unconditional love, you will also learn to love others unconditionally as well.

Forgiving yourself will raise you above strife and conflict — you can observe situations without getting defensive or reacting negatively. You no longer blame other people or situations for what comes into your life, nor do you believe that God is punishing you. In fact, disagreements, arguments and clashes between you and others will all but completely cease. You accept responsibility for who you are, what you do, and what you experience in your life. Worry is practically non-existent because you have learned to control your thinking and live with complete faith in God, knowing without a doubt how much your Creator loves and values you. You have discovered an inner power — the Christ Power within — that carries you through whatever challenges you may meet in life now and in the future.

Since you willingly accept responsibility for your thoughts, actions and reactions, you live life from a deep, inner connection to the Holy Spirit. And you will no longer feel compelled to live your life trying to please others. With the Lord's guidance and love, you joyfully express your unique talents and individuality, humbly recognizing and accepting His guidance in your life.

It's Your Turn! It's time to reclaim yourself from those life-robbing emotions that get stuck in your heart, your mind, and your soul — emotions that continually rake open old wounds. The other person is not what is hurting you. Those old memories and emotions are! It's time to throw them out of your psyche: "Get thee behind me, Satan!"

As a child of God created in His image and likeness, you have a destiny and purpose to fulfill, and only you can live that destiny and purpose. Therefore, right now, determine that you will no longer prevent yourself from knowing and living the marvelous wonder of your being.

THE CAVEAT — RESPONSIBILITY

In Ho'oponopono there is a flip side to the self-forgiveness coin, however, which is that each one of us must take responsibility for what happens in his or her life. Or more correctly, we have to take responsibility for our *experience* of what happens to us — which is simply our interpretation of what happens regardless of whether it actually is good or bad, painful or pleasurable.

That may sound odd but your "experience" of what happens is very personal and subjective. For instance, your friend tells you that her husband said her dress was unattractive. Maybe she has subconscious memories of being ridiculed by siblings or schoolmates, and so she is deeply hurt by his statement, wondering if he finds her ugly, even taking it to the extreme by thinking he doesn't love her anymore. Yet, if there were no subconscious triggers, or if she was aware that her old memories triggered her negative reaction, she would realize that her husband was only criticizing her outfit and not *her* personally. She might even joke that now she has an excuse to buy something new.

It's easier to blame someone else when we're mad or sad or frustrated rather than acknowledging that there is something within *us* that is reacting in an upsetting way. It's easier to blame someone or something else for what is not right in our lives, whether it's our parents, age or education, or any of hundreds of things, rather than accepting that *our* past decisions and *our* choices have brought us to where we are today.

Ho'oponopono helps us examine our feelings, actions and reactions. It helps us recognize what is within us that causes us to react negatively. Then we can take responsibility of our experience of any situation.

We may not believe that we have control over some things that happen to us, but we ultimately have control over our *reactions* to them:

- We can remain in fear and agitation for what "may" happen, or we can remember that we can only live today: *"Sufficient unto the day is the evil thereof."* Matthew 6:34

- We can stay stressed and overwrought during challenging or difficult times, or we can maintain faith that God will see us through any difficulty: *"I can do all things through Christ who strengthens me."* Phil 4:13

- We can stay depressed and beaten over past events or situations, or we can realize that the past is gone and we can enjoy our lives today: *"Remember not the former things, nor consider the things of old."* Isaiah 43:18

Jesus promised us emancipation from fear, agitation, and regrets, though He did not say we would never have them. Yet it is up to us to let go of negative emotions and allow His love to heal us. The purpose of this little book is to give you a valuable tool in Christian Ho'oponopono to learn to honor the beautiful child of God created you to be.

Accepting Responsibility

I now take responsibility for everything that happens to me. That way, I don't have to wait for someone else to change, to apologize to me, or make amends. I don't have to wait for someone else to do something before I can be happy.

By accepting responsibility for what happens to me, I know that I can change what I think, say and do so that I can accomplish and experience what I want in my life.

By controlling my reactions and letting go of habitual negative responses, I simply observe what is happening around me without being caught up in others' "stuff".

I am naturally happy within for I know the love of Christ. No other person controls my happiness or gives me happiness. I don't need anyone else's approval, acceptance, admiration, or love because I approve of myself, I accept myself, and I love myself.

That's it, I can experience whatever it is that I want to experience when I don't require someone else to do something for me first!

HOW TO DO THE CHRISTIAN HO'OPONOPONO FORGIVENESS PRACTICE

Within you is a beautiful, divine child created by God, who is totally unfettered by the "trials and tribulations" of physical life here in the material world. Imagine rising above earthly conflicts. You can see that those trials and tribulations are not a part of your true self. When you release subconscious memories of the pain caused by past and present conflicts and allow the Christ Light to heal you, you will embrace your true identity as that divine child of God.

The Christian Ho'oponopono Forgiveness Practice will gently help you release all pain and torment of past memories and experience the love and forgiveness of the Holy Christ.

There are two ways to practice the Christian Ho'oponopono Forgiveness Practice. The first is in a group setting, the second is when you are alone. Both are equally powerful in allowing you to gently forgive yourself, and embrace that much-needed spiritual healing.

Christian Ho'oponopono Forgiveness Practice for Groups

Materials: Each individual should bring a picture of himself or herself as a child.

Make sure that each person in the group has a picture of himself or herself as a child. It does not make a difference what the age of the child is. If someone has forgotten their picture, they can write their name on a slip of paper and use that instead. There should be one person who facilitates the meditation and does not participate in the actual process.

The participants sit on chairs or on the floor in a circle, and the facilitator begins by explaining what Ho'oponopono ritual is. Each person is told to look at his or her picture and look into the eyes of the child in the photo. Silently or aloud, gently say to this child, "I am sorry. Please forgive me. I love you. Thank you." Repeat the phrase several times as you look at the picture for a minute or so.

The group then passes the picture to the left (or right, the direction does not matter but each person in the group passes in the same direction). Each person then looks at the new picture and repeats the phrases to the child in the photo for up to a minute. The process is repeated until each picture is eventually passed back to its owner.

The participants can then discuss any experiences and feelings they had during the process and the others can give ample support and encouragement for those who are able to express their reactions openly. After everyone has had an opportunity to express any feelings that came up during the exercise, the facilitator gives a closing prayer, explaining that he will recite the prayer in the first person so that each person in the group feels that he or she is praying the prayer. This prayer is to affirm and solidify the cleansing and changes that are initiated in the circle. The facilitator can change or elaborate this prayer as the situation warrants.

Oh Heavenly Father, Precious Savior and Divine Holy Spirit,

I come before you with my heart open to your loving grace. You have long forgiven and forgotten my transgressions from the past to the present and into the future.

I humbly allow your Love and Light to envelop me and cleanse me of guilt, unworthiness, and unneeded emotions and feelings that have held me back from expressing the divine self that I am as your child – created in Grace and Unconditional Love.

I relax and allow the unfolding of your glorious plan in my life and I continually receive your guidance, protection, support, and encouragement in all that I do.

I live to express your Holy Goodness continually.

I give thanks for your blessings and healing. I love myself because I love You and all of your Creation.

In the name of Jesus Christ, my Lord and Savior, Amen

This is a very powerful exercise as each person in the group will have offered forgiveness and unconditional love over your picture, pouring love and healing energy over it. Many, if not all, in the group will sense a shift in attitude, an empowerment and cleansing of guilt, self-condemnation and sadness. At least the process will have started. The facilitator should encourage the participants to repeat the process with their picture regularly and frequently.

Christian Ho'oponopono Forgiveness Practice by yourself:

This beautiful meditation can be done with one or more people. You may use a white candle and a picture of yourself as a child. Soft meditation music, such as Steven Halpern or gentle instrumental hymns, can be played in the background.

Place your picture near the candle. Light the candle and gaze at the flame. Center your attention in your heart. Relax and imagine the presence of the Holy Spirit within you. The candle's flame symbolizes the Divine Presence within.

See your child-self in the picture surrounded in a healing beam of Light that streams down from above. You can imagine the arms of Jesus, God or angels encircling your child-self with healing love and protection. See the Light connecting your own heart with the Christ Light above and around you. Feel the Savior's love streaming from His hands and arms, enveloping you with healing balm, and say to yourself, "I apologize. Please forgive me. I love you. Thank you."

Remember you are saying the words to yourself, not to the Light or God. The Lord has forgiven you already and you only need to accept it in order to let go of guilt, discomfort, and any sense of unworthiness leftover from any past issue. The past is gone and forgotten, it is time to let it go.

See the Light expand to enfold you as you sit in front of the candle. Repeat to yourself, "I apologize. Please forgive me. I love you. Thank you." Breathe deeply and envision toxic emotions flowing out of you as you exhale.

Continue saying, "I love you" and "Thank you" for as long as you need to feel completely free.

By saying, "I apologize. Please forgive me." you are asking *yourself* to forgive you for the hurt and pain you have carried within yourself, for the guilt that you have endured for so long, and for not recognizing and acknowledging the beautiful being that God created.

When you say "I love you," you are saying it to yourself as well as to Jesus. Saying, "I love you" also connects you to the Love and Light of the Savior. You will automatically begin to feel connected to Spirit and resonate and harmonize with His Love and Grace.

"Thank you" expresses your gratitude that healing has occurred and harmony has been restored.

End your Christian Ho'oponopono Forgiveness meditation by praying aloud the following prayer, or one that speaks from your heart. Direct your words to the Christ Light above and around you as you look at the candle flame.

Oh Heavenly Father, Precious Savior and Divine Holy Spirit,

I come before you with my heart open to your loving grace. I know You have long forgiven and forgotten my transgressions from my past to the present, and into the future.

I humbly allow your Love and Light to envelop me and cleanse me of unneeded emotions and feelings that have held me back from expressing the divine self that I am as your child – created in Grace and Unconditional Love.

I relax and allow the unfolding of your glorious plan in my life and continually receive your guidance, protection, support, and encouragement in all that I do.

I live to express your Holy Goodness continually.

I give thanks for your blessings and healing. I love myself because I love You and all of Your Creation.

In the name of Christ our Lord and Savior, Amen

FINAL THOUGHTS

Because of this beautiful Ho'oponopono Forgiveness Practice, that bright, happy child in the picture now sits in a new frame at the front of my dresser. She reminds me each time I look at her that she is — and *I* am — a divine child of God, that she is — and *I* am — loved unconditionally, and that God's Kingdom is a gift for me to use and grow in the glory for which I was made! No longer must I "hide my light under a bushel." No! I live freely and exuberantly; without reservation I love and *expect* love in return because I honor myself and every person I meet. I love myself, not in a vain or superior way, but with gratitude and an awe that I am divinely created, and I express my God-given talents and abilities fearlessly. Because I love myself, I can love others unconditionally, genuinely celebrate their individuality, and heartily encourage their own uniqueness.

Thank you for purchasing this book. I do hope that by using the Christian Ho'oponopono Forgiveness Practice, you can feel the love and comfort of the Lord and Savior Jesus Christ. You are a beautiful child of the Father and you deserve all the blessings that He has promised you.

Yours in His Love and Light
Angela Parish

CONCLUSION

Race Consciousness: Many religions teach of the collective consciousness, or memory, of humanity. All of humanity's thoughts, from the beginning of human creation to the present, aggregate into an invisible thought-cloud surrounding our earth. These memories constitute our "Race," or "Mass Consciousness" or "Race Memories," and are a collection of our pain and suffering from wars, racial hatred, greed and fear. Racial and religious hatred and warfare have continued for hundreds and even thousands of years, and all of these memories have coalesced into the collective consciousness of humankind. These memories affect one's race, culture and society and will remain until they are consciously healed.

On the other hand, our Race Consciousness also includes the higher, spiritual emotions and exaltation that people experience when they come into the presence of Christ or the Holy Spirit. They include emotions engendered when we sincerely help and care for others, or when moved by deep joy and sincere love. The selfless aid that rescue workers give to disaster victims adds an exalted spiritual light to the Race Consciousness. These vibrations work to counteract the powerful negative thought-vibrations of hatred, and this is exactly why we should continue to strive to follow Christ and live in His Love and Light continuously. Many are waiting for Christ to come and save us again, but it is we, individually, who must invite the Savior into our hearts and lead humanity from the brink of self-destruction.

Bring it closer to home: When one practices Ho'oponopono for himself, the process relieves stress and emotional pain, eliminating any personal problems that arise before they become painful memories ingrained in his or her subconscious. Letting go of being a victim, or having to be "right," or wanting revenge toward another person is very difficult to achieve, and using the Christian Ho'oponopono Forgiveness Practice will go far in reclaiming the power that you have given away to these negative emotions.

When you practice the Ho'oponopono technique of repeating, "I'm sorry. Please forgive me. I love you. Thank you," you remove the other person from the conflict, taking full responsibility for your emotions, feelings and reactions. You stop blaming the other person and, instead, seek those triggers within yourself that react to the other person's actions or words. When you shift your focus to only your feelings and reactions, you resolve them within yourself and the situation inevitably, often instantly, disappears.

It may take years of practice but the results are well worth the effort.

~ ~ ~

Thank you for purchasing and reading this book. If you enjoyed it and feel that you received value from it, I'd like to ask you to take a moment and leave a review on Amazon. Simply type the following address into the address bar, and it will take you directly to the review page:

amzn.to/1nMJh0n

And please consider sharing it on Facebook and Twitter. Your reviews help me reach more people.

Sincerely,
Angela Parish

OTHER PRODUCTS BY ANGELA PARISH

If you enjoyed Christian Ho'oponopono, you may also enjoy *Christian Transformation: Embracing the Power of Christ through the Holy Spirit* — a 7-day video journey of renewal and transformation that will instill within you the Truth that Jesus Christ came to teach us that:

- You are a divine child of God
- You are forgiven
- God loves you unconditionally
- You are worthy to receive all of God's blessings

Available on DVD (formatted for U.S. DVD players only), or download them or stream them on your computer.

Download a free video from the series at:

www.mychristpower.com.

ABOUT THE AUTHOR

Angela Parish grew up in a small town hearing mixed messages in church. Her Sunday school teachers told the children of God's love, how Jesus forgives and loves children unconditionally, and that the Holy Spirit is always with them. Yet, the minister would preach about the evils of man, the sinful nature of everyone, and how you will burn in Hell if you do not repent your evil ways.

Angela studied the words of Jesus to try and understand His true message. She heard adults pray, but not like Jesus taught when He told us to pray as if you have already received that for which you have prayed. Instead, they would tell God how sinful and undeserving they were, and then fearfully ask Him for a blessing.

Angela did not feel particularly sinful — surely God understood the temptations of a little girl — and she also knew that Jesus forgave sinners who accepted them into their lives. From a very young age, she felt close to the Holy Spirit, to angels and to Jesus, and never feared God. She wondered why adults did not practice what they taught. She felt safe within her private world, but was often afraid of others' mean spiritedness in the outer world of school, and later adult society.

Partly because of religious mixed messages, and partly because of wounds from unkind words she heard from others, Angela suffered from a deep lack of self-esteem. She found it difficult to excel among her peers; she would shrink back from opportunities to share her unique talents and abilities. Having only a few close friends, she spent many hours alone with her thoughts and her invisible angels.

When Angela was a young adult, she was fortunate enough to move in with her beloved grandmother while attending a local community college. Her grandmother was a wise and deeply spiritual woman who taught Angela how to experience God's unlimited love; how to understand what Jesus meant when He said, "It is done unto you as you believe"; and how to apply His teachings in her life. Her grandmother gently and lovingly guided her in learning to "pray as if you have already received that for which you pray," and the true meaning of "pride goeth before a fall."

Angela's grandmother taught her many spiritual "secrets," teachings not taught in church. These included using the healing power of the White Light of Christ and how to tap into this Christ Power to follow God's Word.

Years later, as a church pianist, Angela again would hear most of the parishioners talk of their unworthiness to receive God's many blessings, and also stay focused on their trials and tribulations and transgressions. It was then that she decided to start teaching the beautiful message of Christ's Love. She realized that she had to share the lessons she had learned from her beloved grandmother.

All of Angela's life experiences have led up to her mission of teaching a positive Christianity. She wants all of humanity to understand and know that we must take responsibility for what we have created in this world through the mass consciousness of greed, fear, guilt, covetousness and hatred, and that it is up to Christians and those who seek relationship with God to infuse our mass consciousness with spiritual Love, Light and Peace.

Please visit Angela's websites www.christianhooponopono.com and www.mychristpower.com to learn more about positive Christianity and the deeper teachings her grandmother taught her.

BONUS

Visit **www.christianhooponopono.com**
and download the free mp3* of the
Christian Ho'oponopono Forgiveness Meditation
In addition, you will receive the free Bonus Report:
"Meditation for Christians"

Christian Ho'oponopono –
Your Key to Self-Forgiveness,
Release from Guilt, Fear, and Anger,
and Finding Inner Peace

**Free Audio
Forgiveness Meditation**

*This is a free audio and no credit card is required

Printed in Great Britain
by Amazon